JAMAICA BAY   EVOLVING EDGES

JAMAICA BAY PAMPHLET LIBRARY 11

JAMAICA BAY
EVOLVING EDGES

STRUCTURES OF COASTAL RESILIENCE

Jamaica Bay Team
Spitzer School of Architecture
The City College of New York

Catherine Seavitt Nordenson, editor
Associate Professor of Landscape Architecture

Kjirsten Alexander
Research Associate

Danae Alessi
Research Associate

Eli Sands
Research Assistant

JAMAICA BAY PAMPHLET LIBRARY
11 Jamaica Bay   Evolving Edges

ISBN 978-1-942900-11-5

COPYRIGHT

CONTACT

Catherine Seavitt Nordenson
cseavittnordenson@ccny.cuny.edu
www.structuresofcoastalresilience.org

SCR Jamaica Bay Team
The City College of New York
Spitzer School of Architecture
Program in Landscape Architecture, Room 2M24A
141 Convent Avenue New York, New York 10031

COVER

Historic Edges and Channels, 1879 - 2011.
data source: NOAA

supported by

SHORELINE 1879
CHANNELS 1879
MUDFLATS 1879
INFRASTRUCTURE 1879
RAILROAD 1879

1879

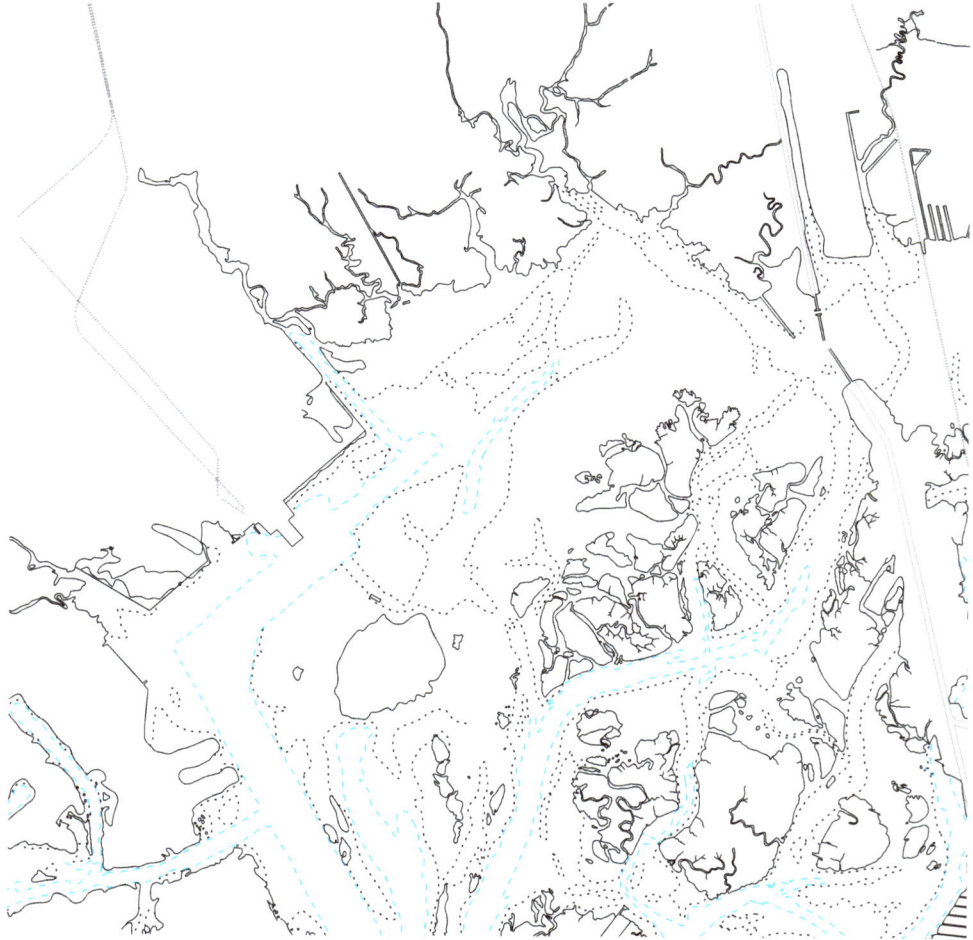

SHORELINE 1929
CHANNELS 1929
MUDFLATS 1929
INFRASTRUCTURE 1929
RAILROAD 1929

1929

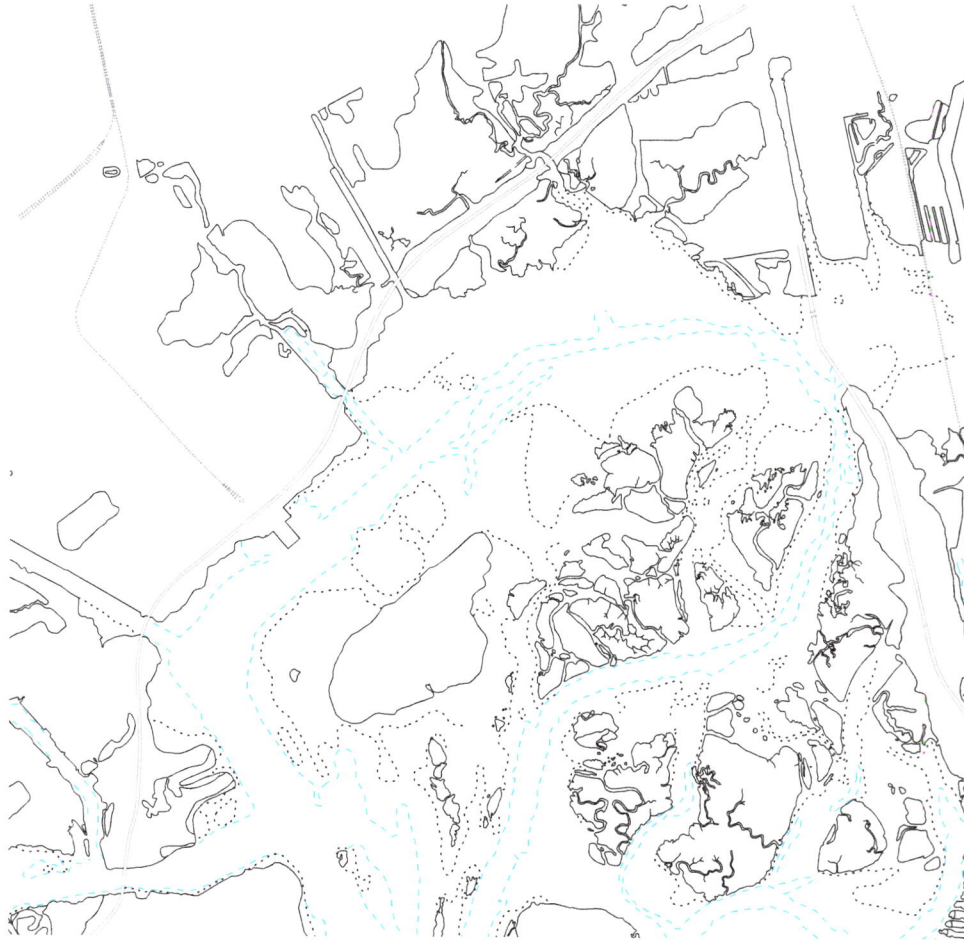

SHORELINE 1948
CHANNELS 1948
MUDFLATS 1948
INFRASTRUCTURE 1948
RAILROAD 1948

1948

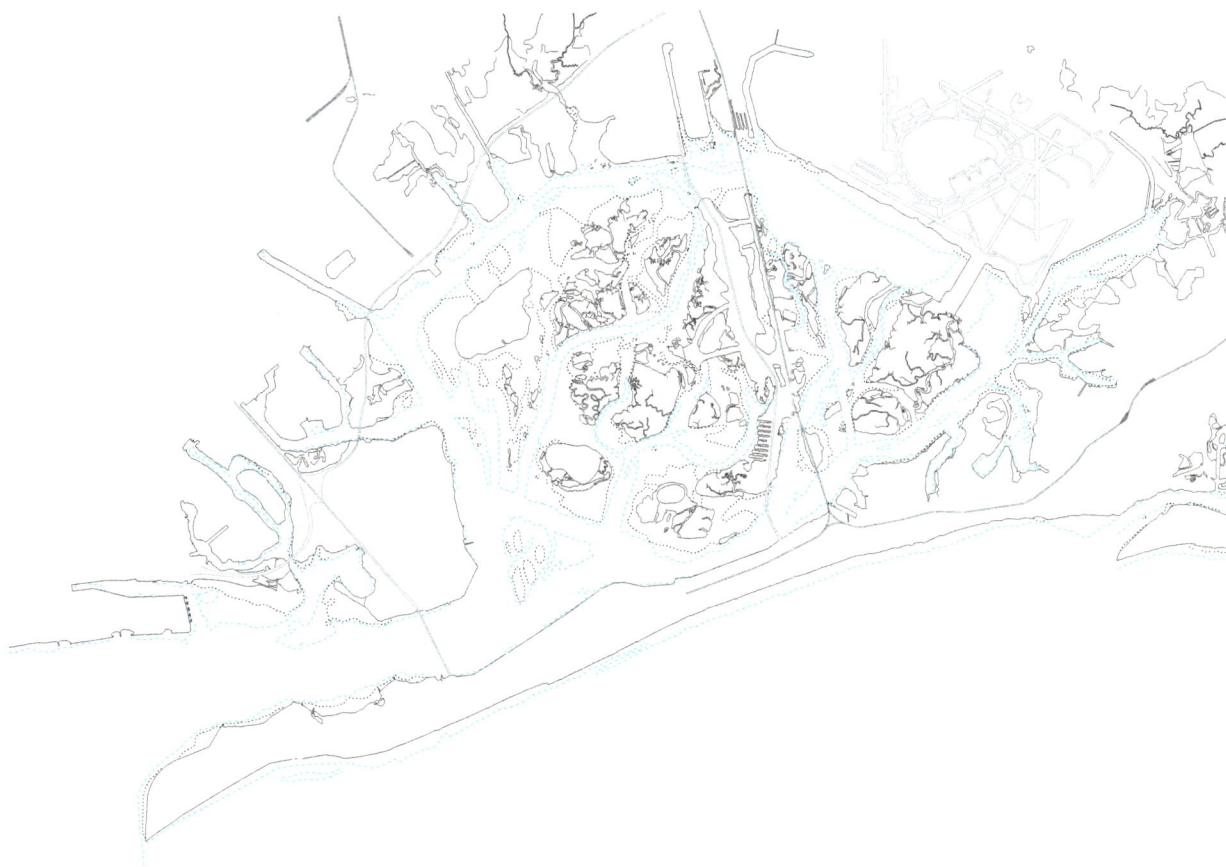

SHORELINE 1965
CHANNELS 1965
MUDFLATS 1965
INFRASTRUCTURE 1965
RAILROAD 1965

1965

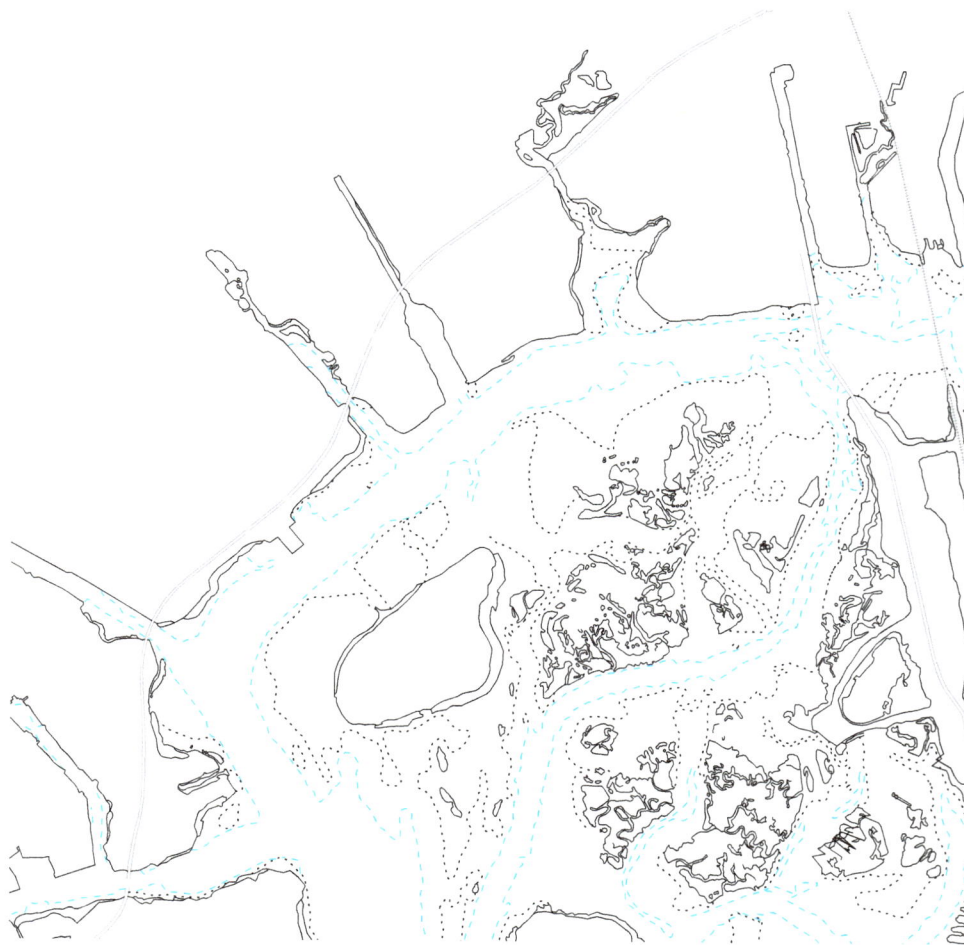

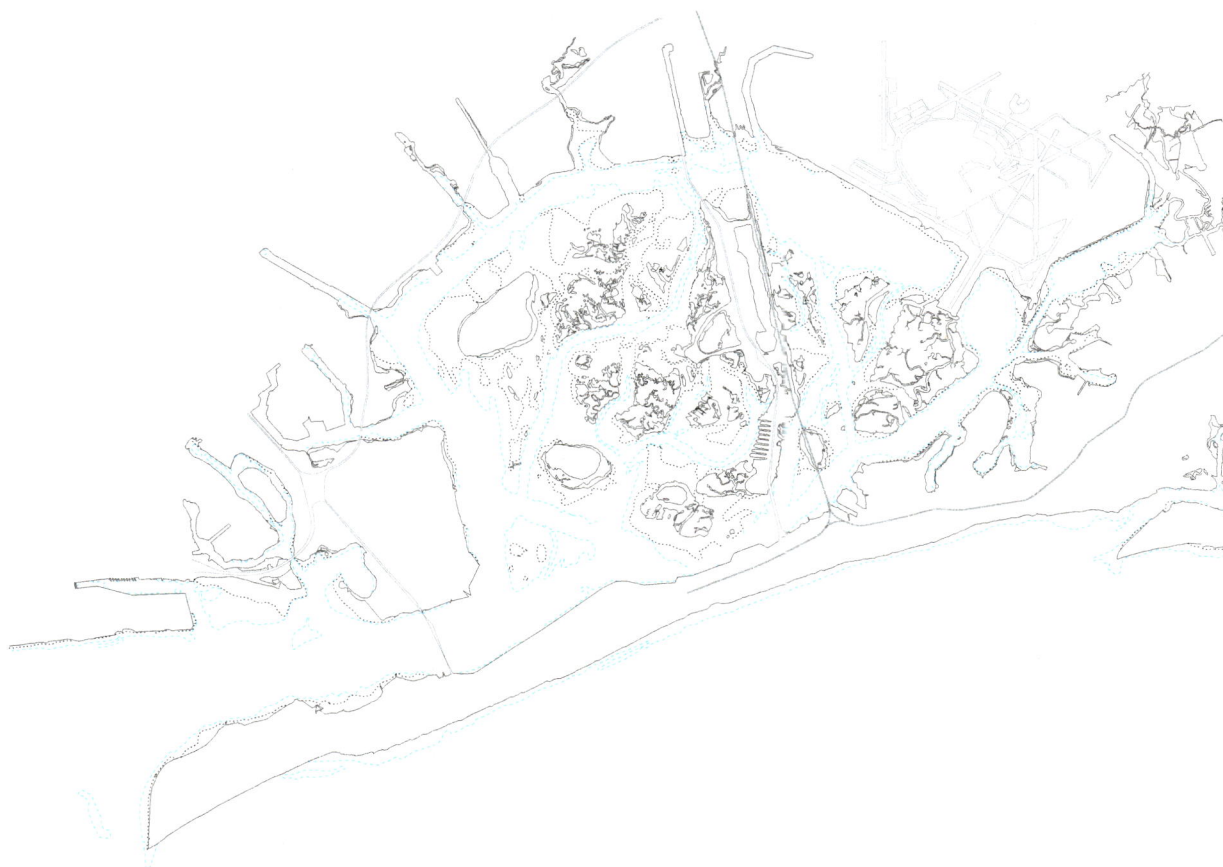

SHORELINE 1985
CHANNELS 1985
MUDFLATS 1985
INFRASTRUCTURE 1985
RAILROAD 1985

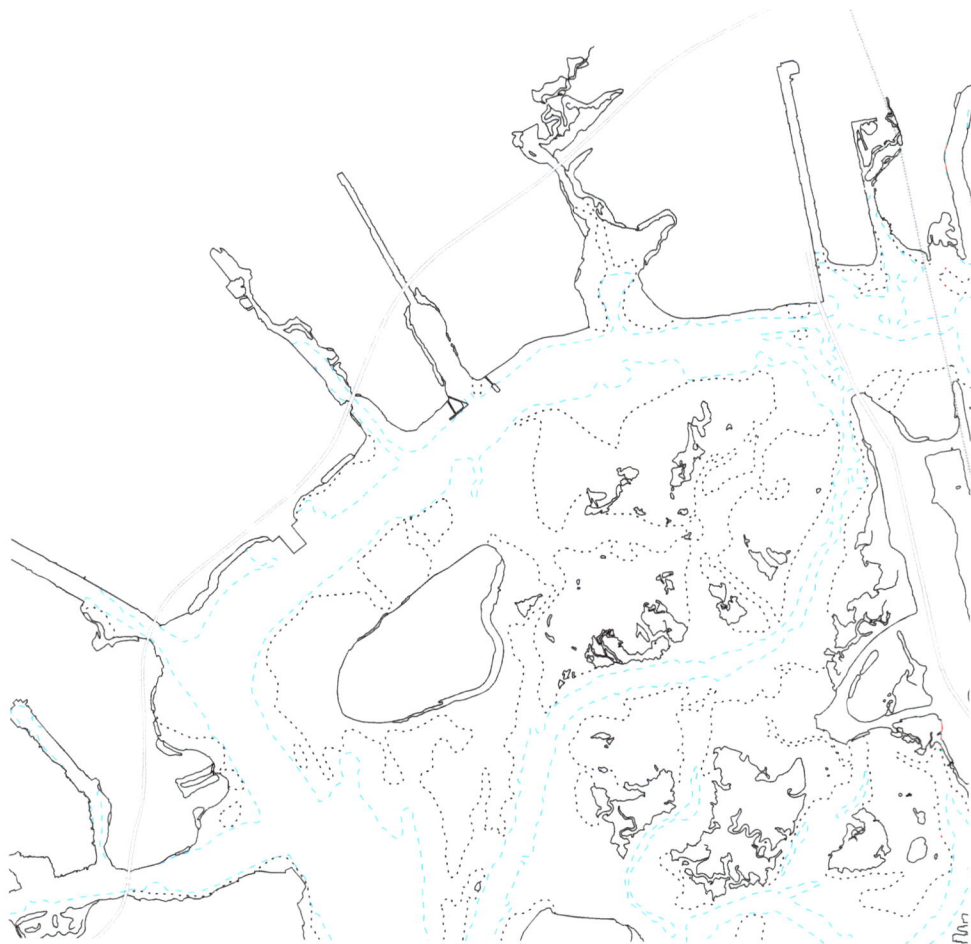

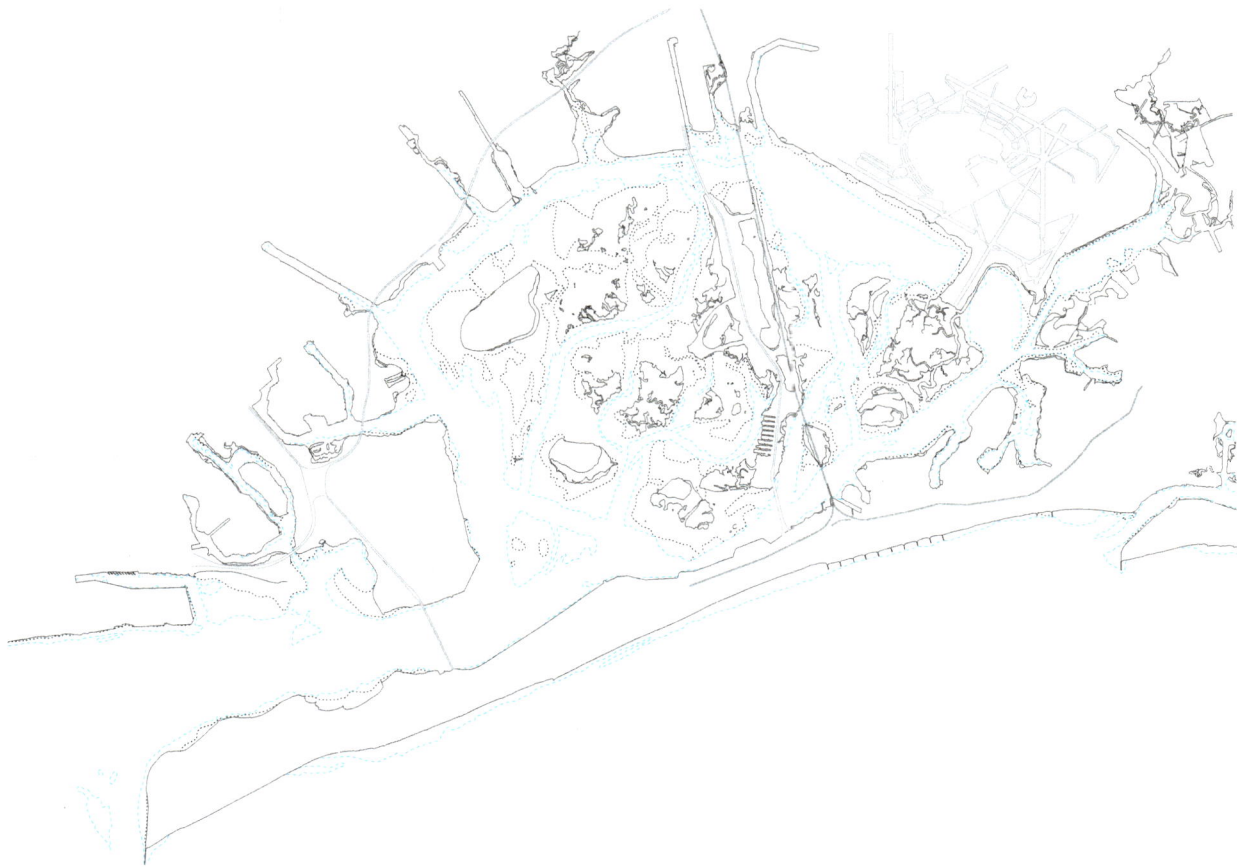

SHORELINE 2011
CHANNELS 2011
MUDFLATS 2011
INFRASTRUCTURE 2011
RAILROAD 2011

2011

1879

1929

1948

1965

1985

2011

SHORELINE 2011
SHORELINE 1985
SHORELINE 1965
SHORELINE 1948
SHORELINE 1929
SHORELINE 1879

Shoreline evolution overlay 1879 - 2011

1879

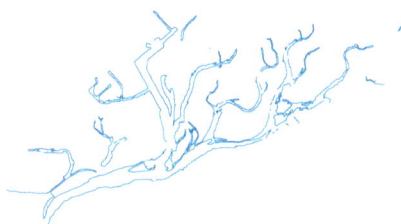

1929

1948

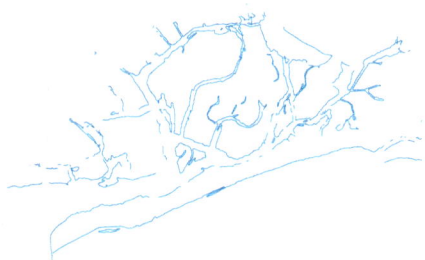

1965

1985

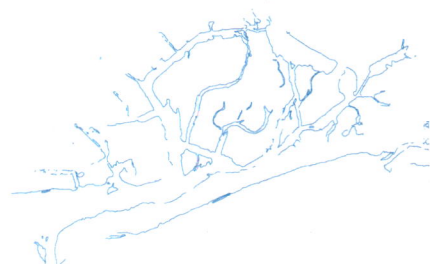

2011

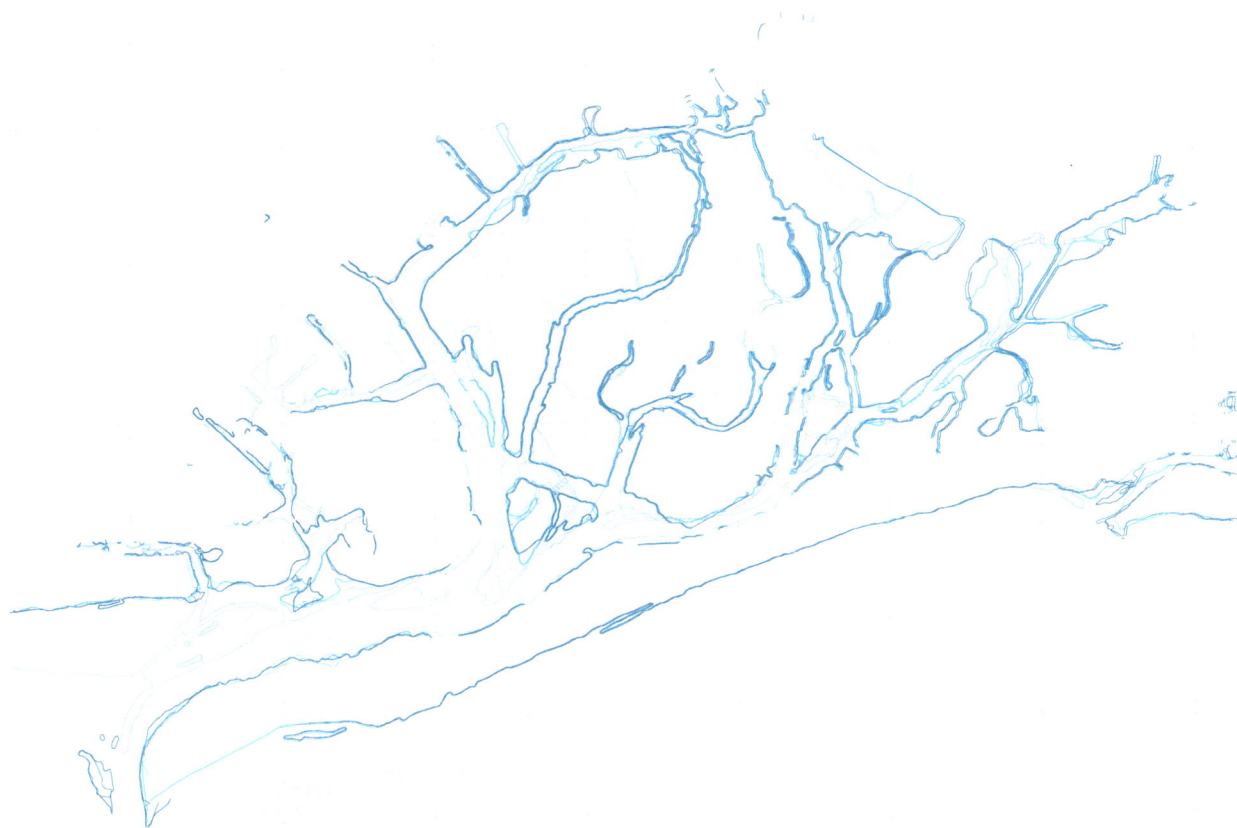

Channel evolution overlay 1879 - 2011

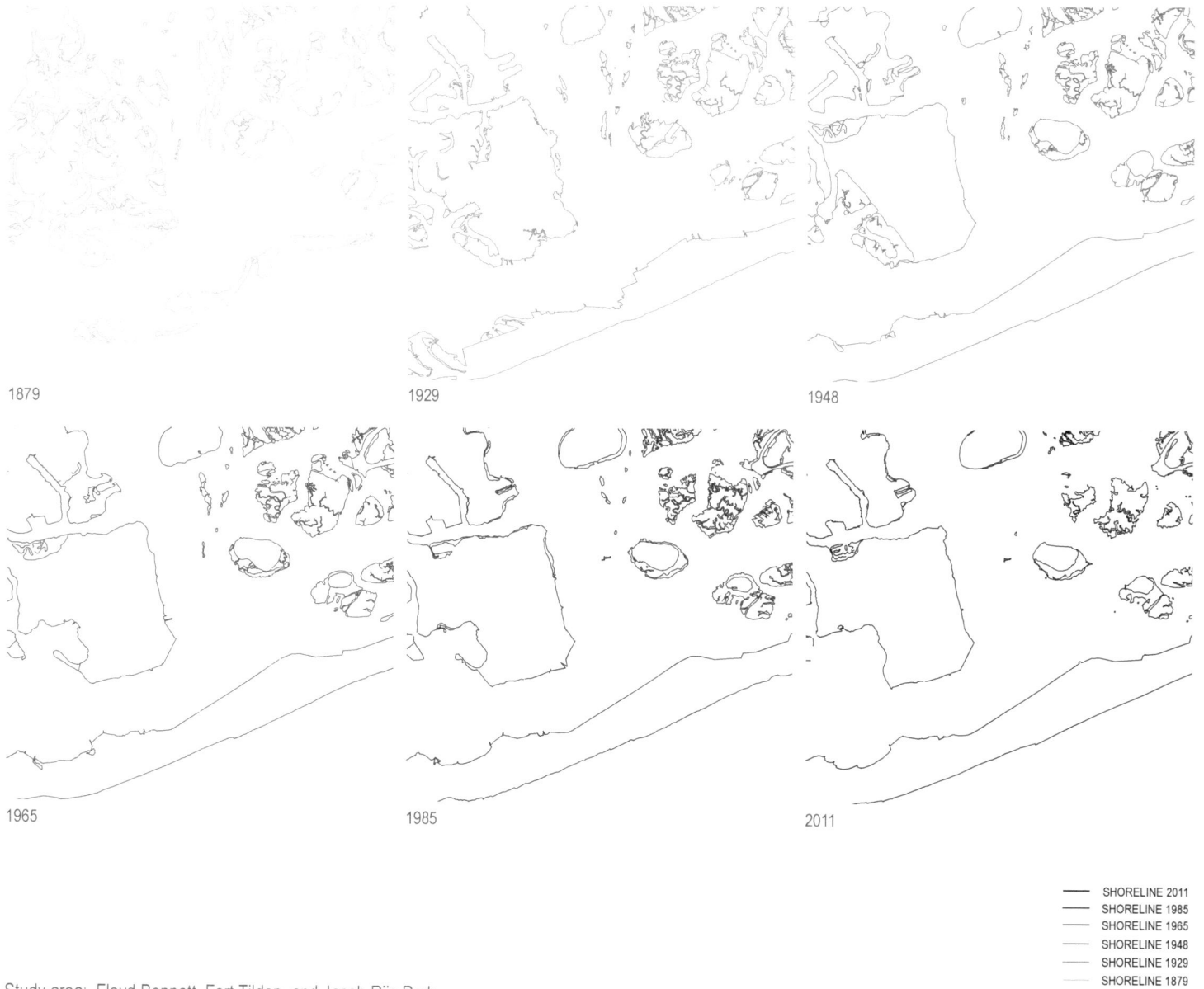

1879

1929

1948

1965

1985

2011

Study area: Floyd Bennett, Fort Tilden, and Jacob Riis Park

SHORELINE 2011
SHORELINE 1985
SHORELINE 1965
SHORELINE 1948
SHORELINE 1929
SHORELINE 1879

Shoreline evolution overlay 1879 - 2011

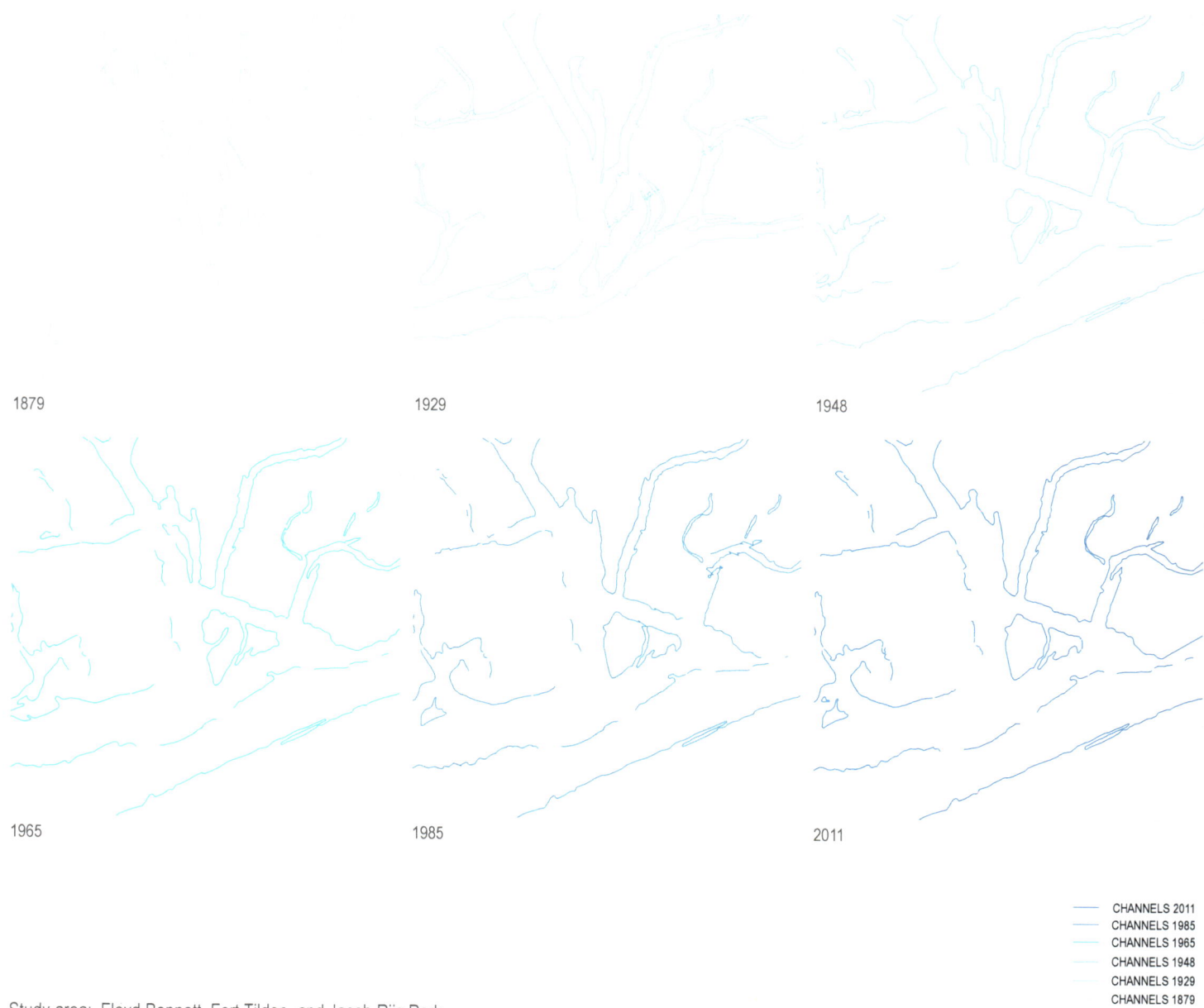

1879

1929

1948

1965

1985

2011

CHANNELS 2011
CHANNELS 1985
CHANNELS 1965
CHANNELS 1948
CHANNELS 1929
CHANNELS 1879

Study area: Floyd Bennett, Fort Tilden, and Jacob Riis Park

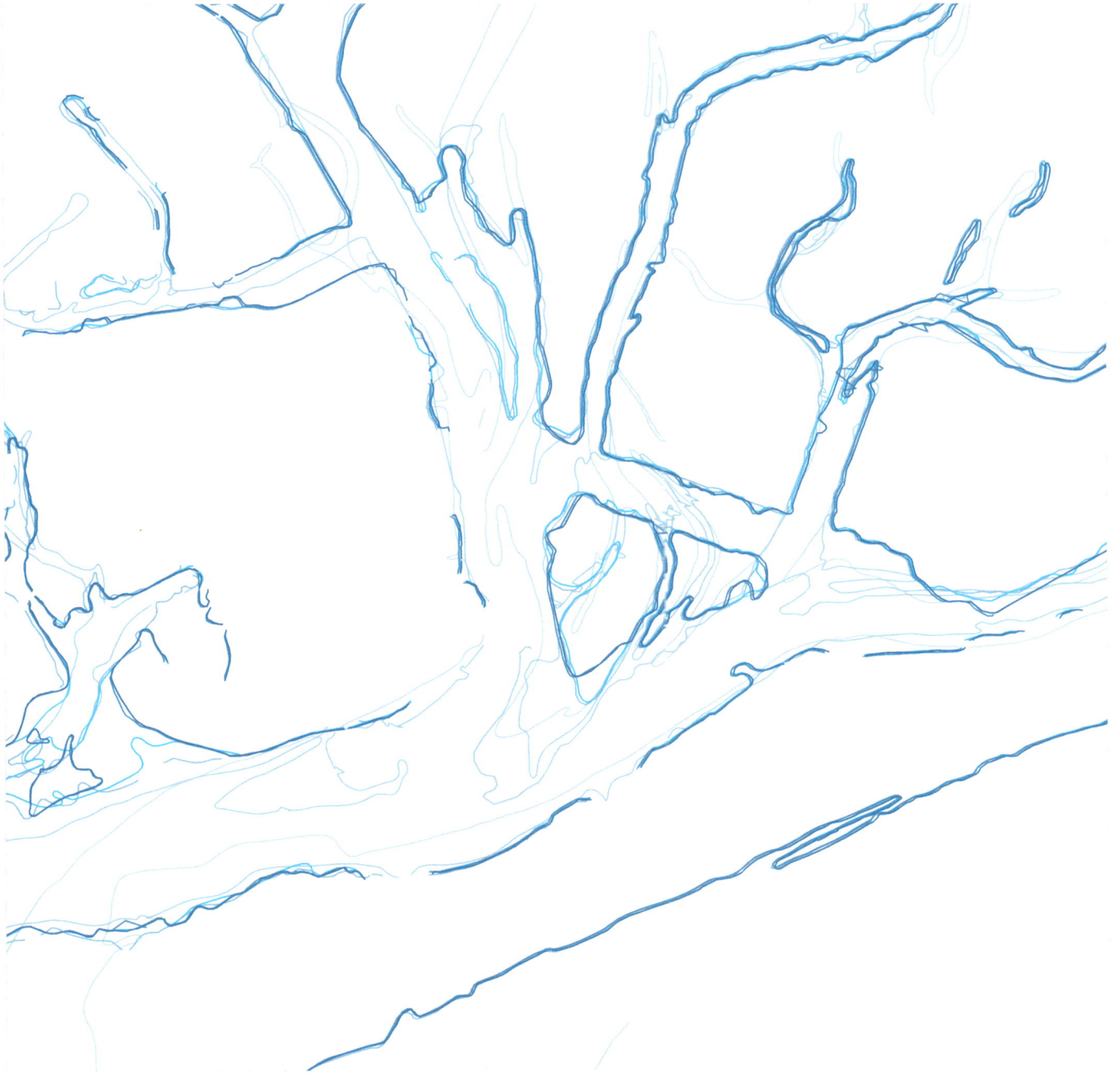

Channel evolution overlay 1879 - 2011

1879

1929

1948

1965

1985

2011

	SHORELINE 2011
	SHORELINE 1985
	SHORELINE 1965
	SHORELINE 1948
	SHORELINE 1929
	SHORELINE 1879

Study area: Mill Basin, Canarsie, and Howard Beach

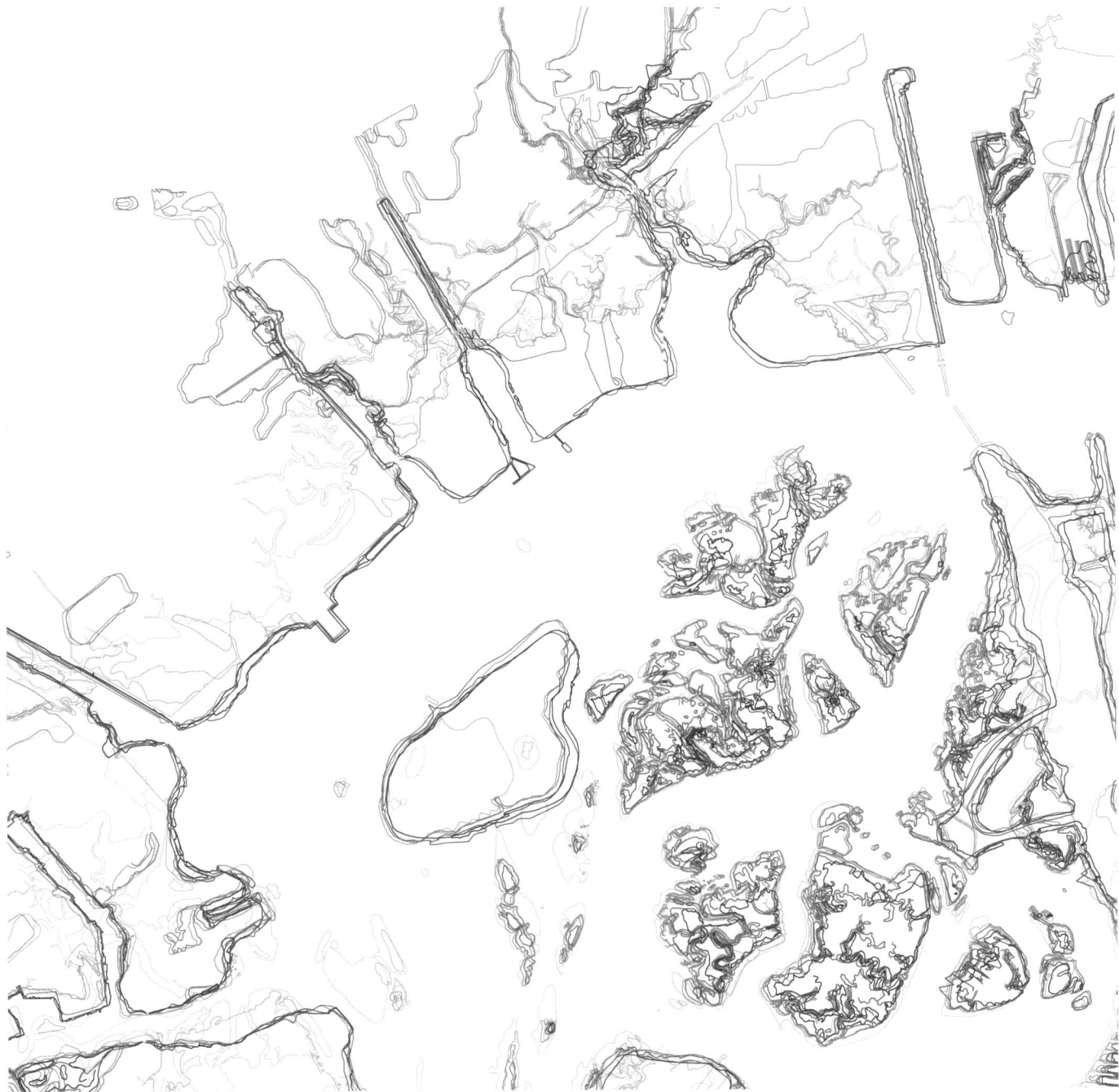

Shoreline evolution overlay 1879 - 2011

28

1879

1929

1948

1965

1985

2011

CHANNELS 2011
CHANNELS 1985
CHANNELS 1965
CHANNELS 1948
CHANNELS 1929
CHANNELS 1879

Study area: Mill Basin, Canarsie, and Howard Beach

Channel evolution overlay 1879 - 2011

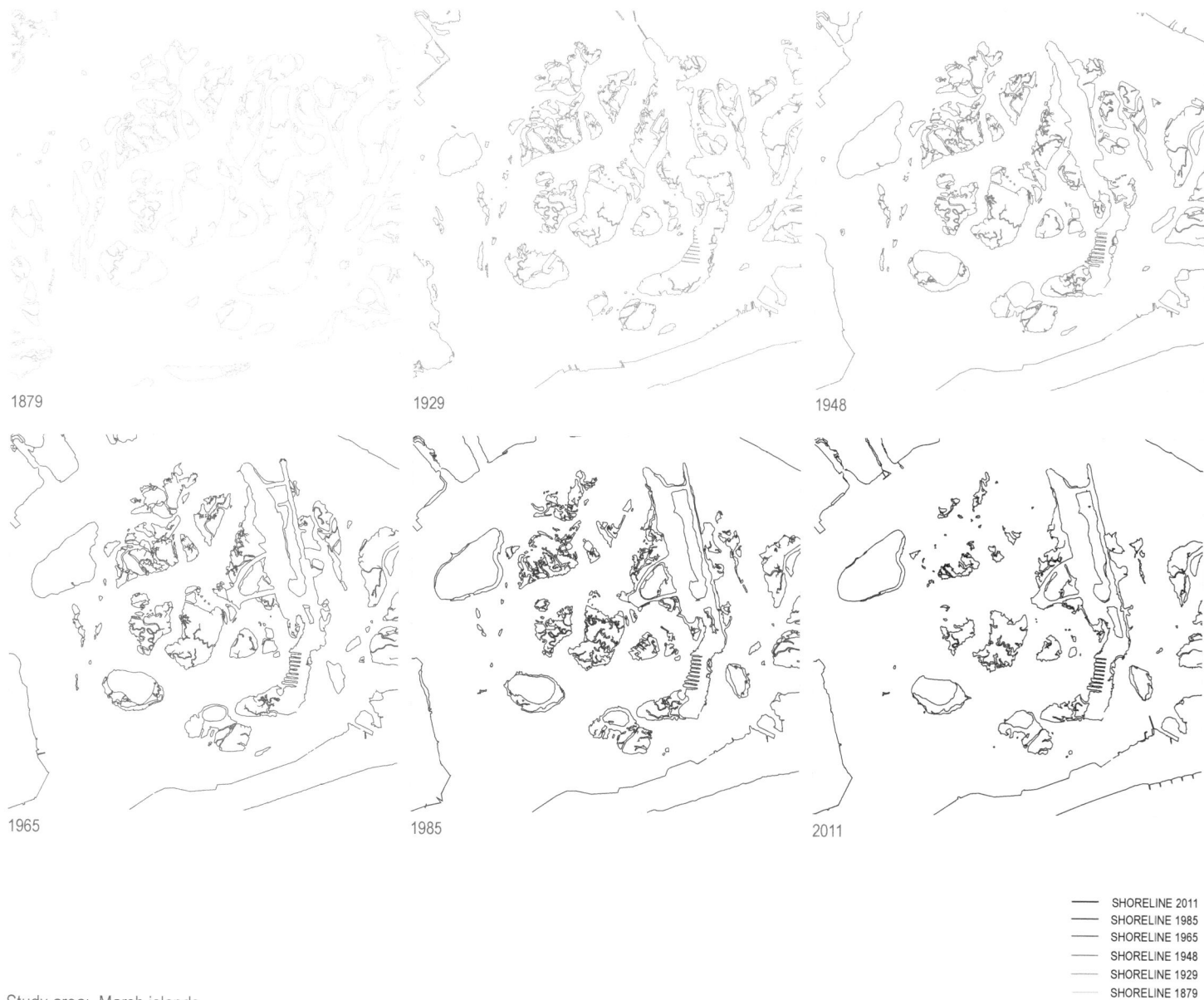

1879

1929

1948

1965

1985

2011

Study area: Marsh islands

SHORELINE 2011
SHORELINE 1985
SHORELINE 1965
SHORELINE 1948
SHORELINE 1929
SHORELINE 1879

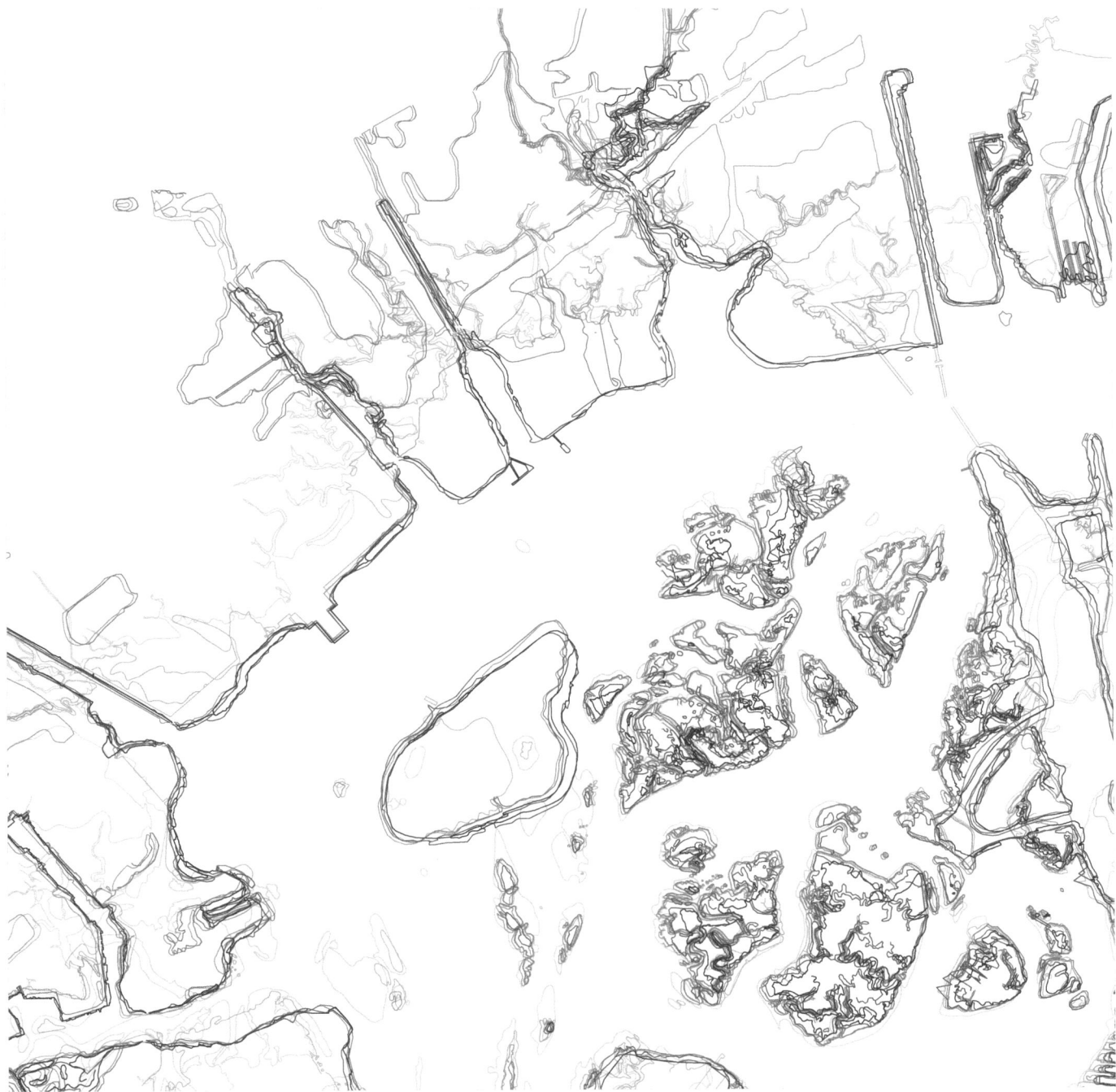

Shoreline evolution overlay 1879 - 2011

1879

1929

1948

1965

1985

2011

Study area: Marsh islands

CHANNELS 2011
CHANNELS 1985
CHANNELS 1965
CHANNELS 1948
CHANNELS 1929
CHANNELS 1879

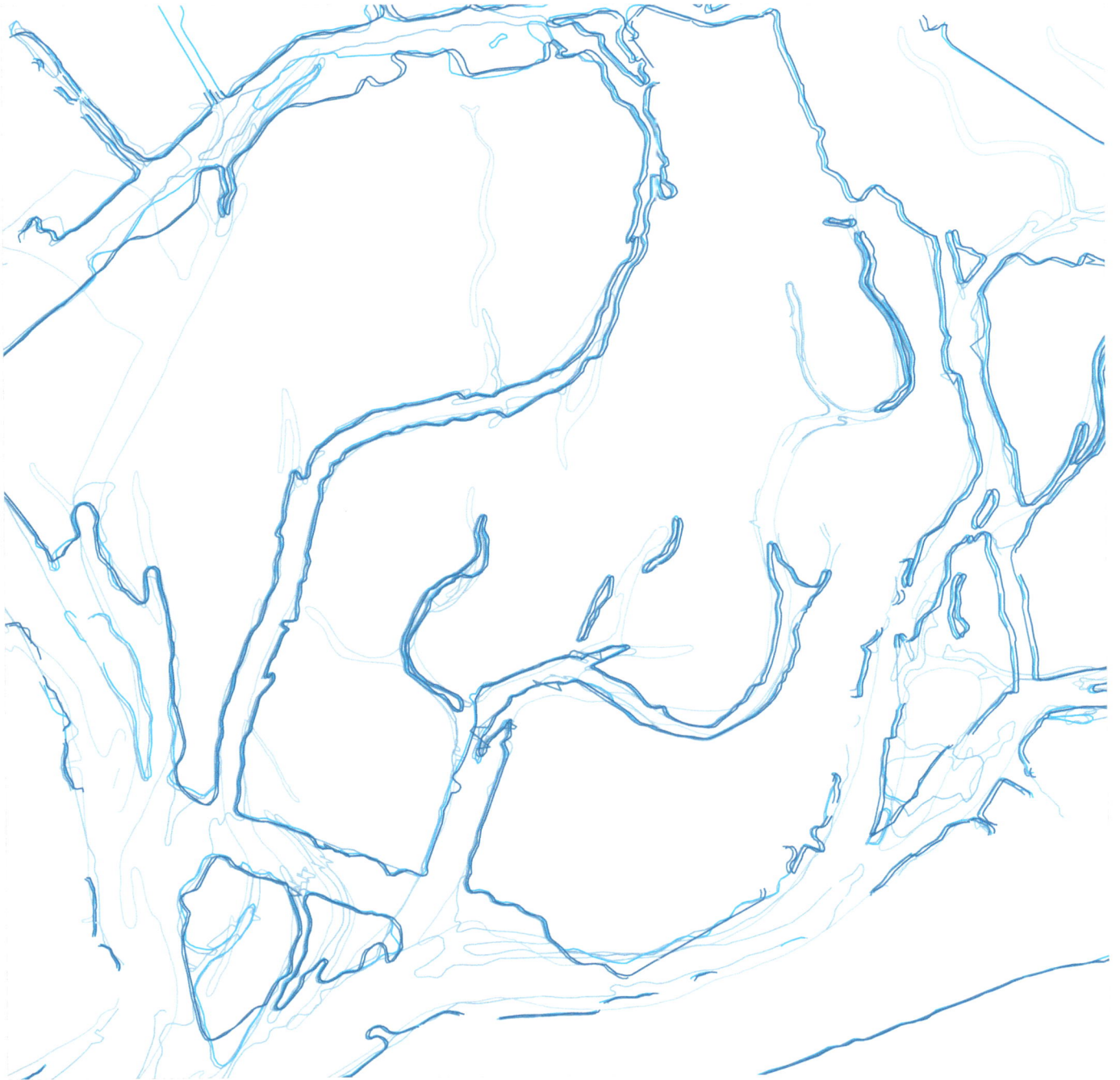

Channel evolution overlay 1879 - 2011

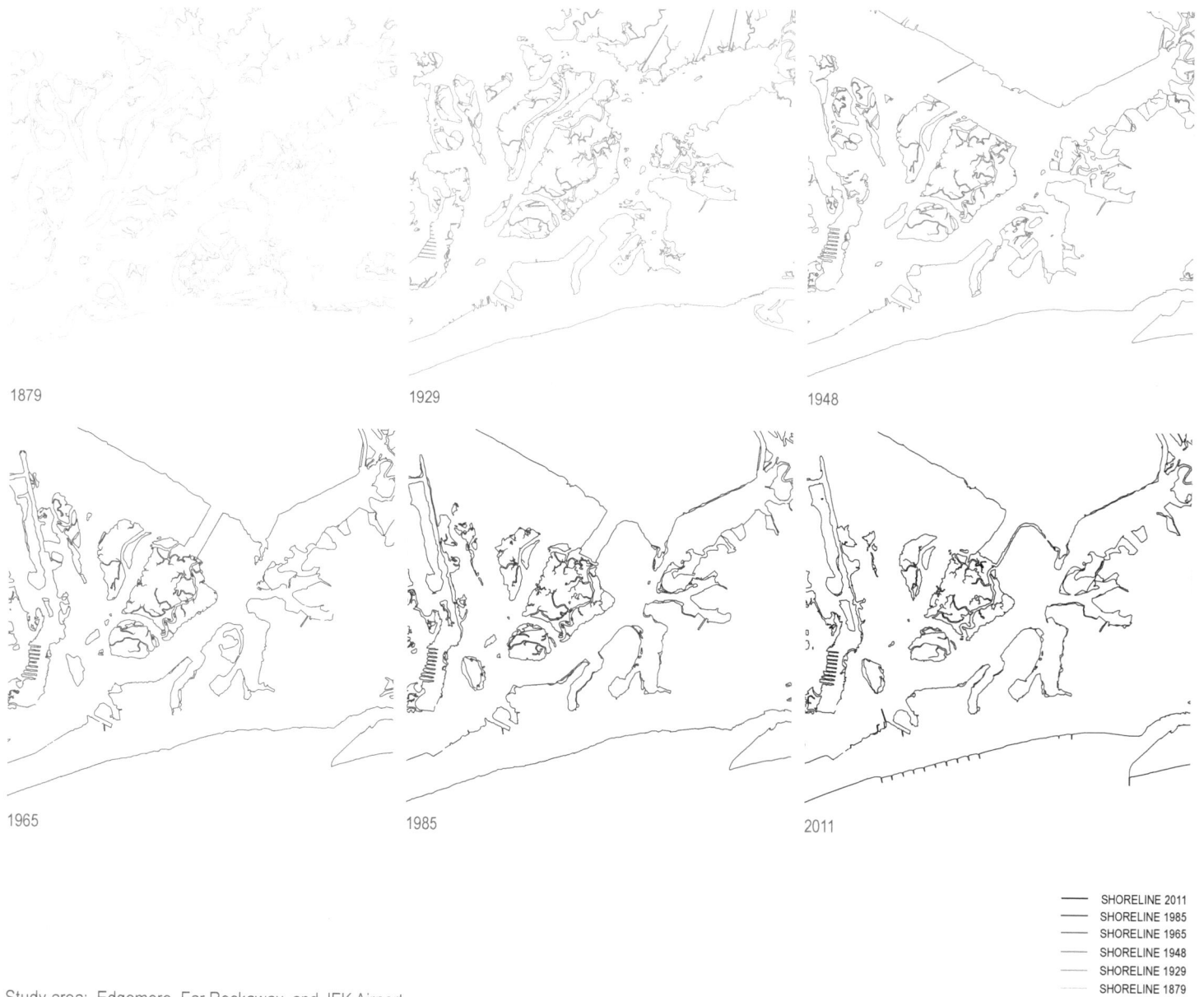

1879

1929

1948

1965

1985

2011

Study area: Edgemere, Far Rockaway, and JFK Airport

SHORELINE 2011
SHORELINE 1985
SHORELINE 1965
SHORELINE 1948
SHORELINE 1929
SHORELINE 1879

Shoreline evolution overlay 1879 - 2011

36

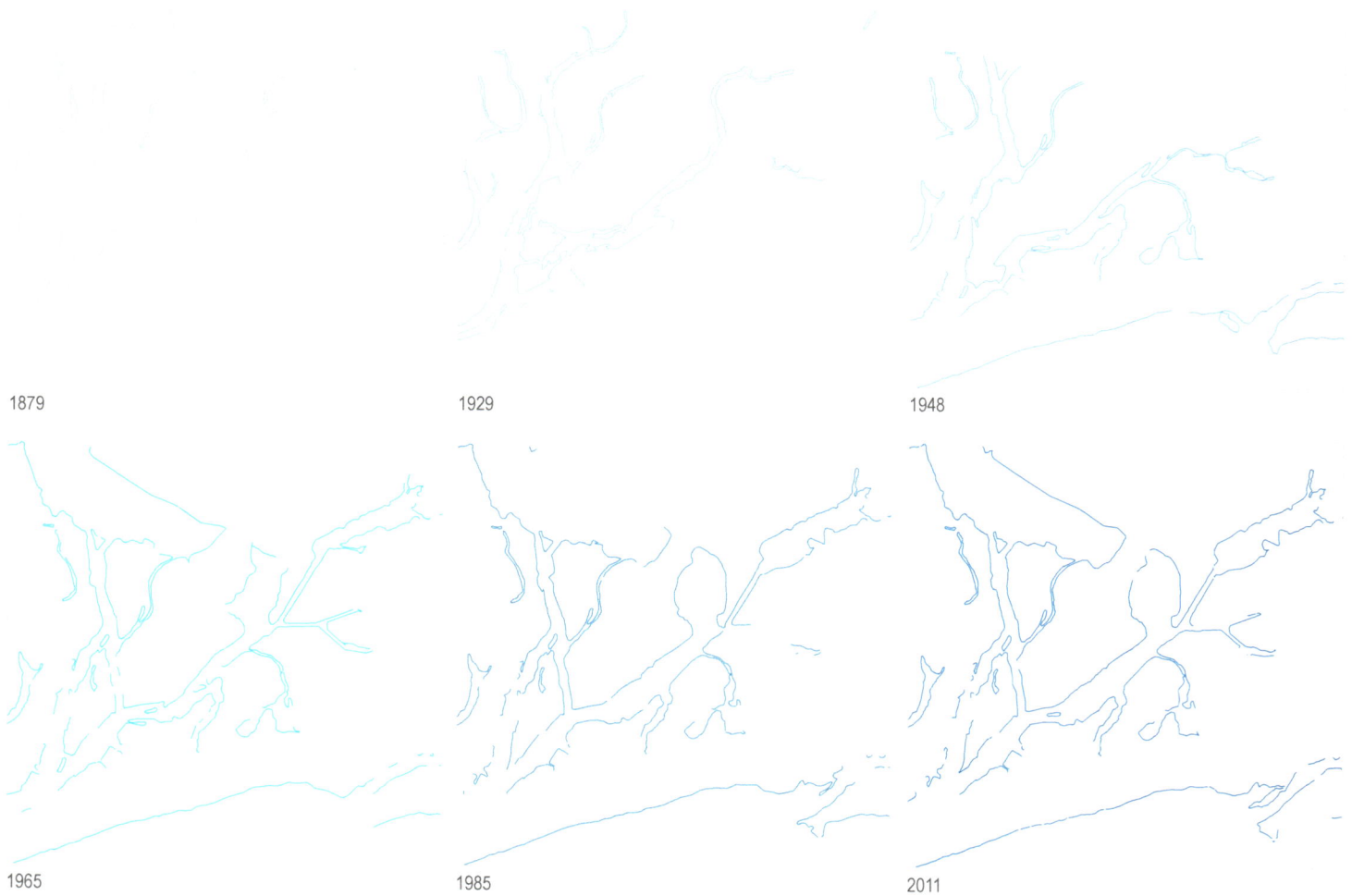

1879

1929

1948

1965

1985

2011

CHANNELS 2011
CHANNELS 1985
CHANNELS 1965
CHANNELS 1948
CHANNELS 1929
CHANNELS 1879

Study area: Edgemere, Far Rockaway, and JFK Airport

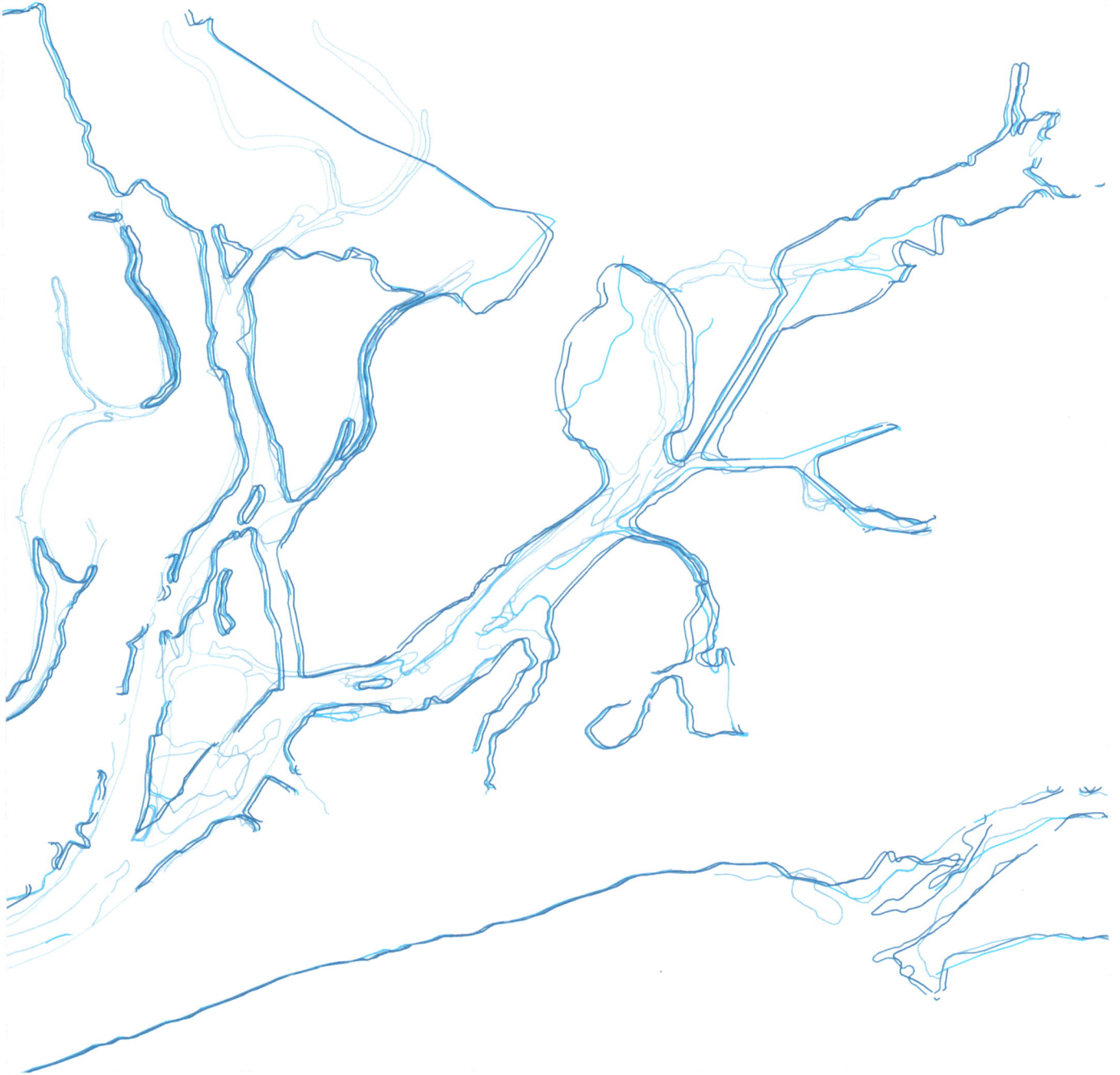

Channel evolution overlay 1879 - 2011

www.ingramcontent.com/pod-product-compliance
Lightning Source LLC
Chambersburg PA
CBHW060827270326
41931CB00002B/83